United States Government Accountability Office

Report to Congressional Requesters

I0448620

July 2013

FOREIGN AFFAIRS MANAGEMENT

State Department Has Strengthened Foreign Service Promotion Process Internal Controls, but Documentation Gaps Remain

July 2013

GAO Highlights

Highlights of GAO-13-654, a report to congressional requesters.

FOREIGN AFFAIRS MANAGEMENT

State Department Has Strengthened Foreign Service Promotion Process Internal Controls, but Documentation Gaps Remain

Why GAO Did This Study

State's Foreign Service promotion process follows an up-or-out principle, under which failure to gain promotion to higher rank within a specified time leads to mandatory retirement for personnel in certain occupational categories. State's OIG and the Foreign Service Grievance Board identified procedural concerns relating to the process in 2010.

GAO was asked to review the Foreign Service promotion process. This report examines (1) State's process for ranking and promoting Foreign Service personnel, (2) procedural changes State has made to its Foreign Service promotion process in response to identified concerns, and (3) the extent to which updated procedures were consistently followed in 2011 and 2012 and whether any notable concerns about the promotion process remain. GAO reviewed laws and procedures; analyzed selection, performance standards, and reconstituted board files as well as grievance case files for the 2011 and 2012 promotion cycles; interviewed State officials; and contacted 2011 and 2012 board members to offer them an opportunity to comment on the process.

What GAO Recommends

GAO recommends that State take actions to ensure full implementation of promotion process internal controls. State concurred with GAO's recommendation.

View GAO-13-654. For more information, contact Michael J. Courts at (202) 512-8980 or courtsm@gao.gov.

What GAO Found

The Department of State's (State) Foreign Service promotion process includes convening several types of boards to evaluate candidates for promotion and identify other candidates for possible separation from the Service. State has a separate process to address related grievances. Selection boards review all candidates and sort them into one of three categories: promotable, mid-ranked, and low-ranked. The selection boards produce rank-ordered lists of those candidates recommended for promotion, and a "cut line" is subsequently determined based on the number of available promotion slots. Before announcing promotions, State vets all recommended candidates to determine whether there are outstanding issues, such as a pending investigation, that can lead to their removal from the promotion list. Subsequently, State convenes performance standards boards to assess low-ranked candidates for possible separation from the Service. There are several mechanisms to address grievances relating to the promotion process. For example, State may initiate reconstituted boards to reassess candidates if a board failed to follow the procedures or if the underlying performance information contained omissions or inaccuracies. Employees not satisfied with grievance outcomes can file an appeal with the Foreign Service Grievance Board.

In response to concerns identified by the Office of Inspector General (OIG) and Foreign Service Grievance Board in 2010, State has taken a number of actions to strengthen its Foreign Service promotion process internal controls. For example, in response to concerns about improper introduction of information about candidates, State instituted a requirement that board members sign an oath to adhere to the promotion criteria and protect the confidentiality of board materials. State also revised its procedures governing recusal requests, thereby broadening the provisions under which a candidate can request an individual board member's recusal from reviewing their file. In addition, State updated its reconstituted board procedures, outlining a set of required documents, such as signed board member score sheets, to be included in each board's official record. In addition to actions taken in response to others' identified concerns, State initiated other practices to strengthen promotion process safeguards, such as including selection board and reconstituted board member recusal memos in the final board report.

GAO found that Foreign Service selection boards, performance standards boards, and reconstituted boards complied with many of State's updated procedures in the 2011 and 2012 Foreign Service promotion cycles, but some board reports had documentation gaps for certain internal controls. For example, all 41 selection board reports we reviewed included a signed memo certifying final results. However, only 29 of 41 selection boards had signed oaths from all board members, and 45 of 122 required oaths were missing from 2012 selection board reports. In addition, some board reports lacked documentation of some recusal requests. The absence of a fully documented system of controls increases the risk that intentional or unintentional failures to implement safeguards, by board members or State Human Resources staff, may go undetected and uncorrected. Such a failure to implement safeguards, in turn, increases the risk that the integrity of promotion results could be intentionally or inadvertently compromised.

_____ United States Government Accountability Office

Contents

Abbreviations

AFSA	American Foreign Service Association
HR	Bureau of Human Resources
State	Department of State
OIG	Department of State Office of Inspector General
Director General	Director General of the Foreign Service and Director of Human Resources
EER	Employee Evaluation Report
FAM	Foreign Affairs Manual

GAO U.S. GOVERNMENT ACCOUNTABILITY OFFICE

441 G St. N.W.
Washington, DC 20548

July 18, 2013

The Honorable Ed Royce
Chairman
The Honorable Eliot L. Engel
Ranking Member
Committee on Foreign Affairs
House of Representatives

The Honorable Ileana Ros-Lehtinen
House of Representatives

The Department of State (State) assessed more than 8,500 Foreign Service personnel performance files for the 2012 promotion process. State's Foreign Service promotion system follows an up-or-out principle, under which failure to gain promotion to a higher rank within a specified period for certain personnel leads to mandatory retirement. Key aspects of State's promotion process include the annual convening of selection boards, State's processing of selection board results, and the convening of performance standards boards to determine whether "low ranked" officers should be recommended for separation from the Foreign Service. Subsequent to previous allegations of improprieties in the process, State's Office of Inspector General (OIG) reviewed State's Foreign Service promotion process and concluded, in March 2010, that it was fundamentally fair and trustworthy.[1] Nonetheless, the OIG identified areas of concern and made recommendations to strengthen the process, which State agreed to implement.

You asked us to examine State's Foreign Service promotion process in light of previously identified concerns. This report addresses actions taken by State since March 2010 to help ensure the Foreign Service promotion process operates with fairness and integrity. Specifically, this report examines (1) State's process for ranking and promoting Foreign Service personnel, (2) procedural changes State has made to its Foreign Service promotion process in response to identified concerns, and (3) the

---

[1]United States Department of State and the Broadcasting Board of Governors Office of Inspector General, *Review of the Integrity and Fairness of the Foreign Service Selection Board Process*, ISP-I-10-47 (Washington, D.C.: March 2010). The report focused on the 2004 to 2008 promotion cycles.

extent to which updated procedures were consistently followed in 2011 and 2012 and whether any notable concerns about the promotion process remain.

To review State's process for ranking and promoting Foreign Service personnel, we reviewed relevant laws, regulations, and procedures governing State's promotion and grievance processes, and interviewed officials from State's Bureau of Human Resources (HR). We reviewed State data on the 2011 and 2012 Foreign Service promotion cycles. We reviewed how these data were collected, entered, and checked for accuracy, and determined them to be sufficiently reliable for our purposes. To examine the procedural changes State has made to its Foreign Service promotion process, we reviewed concerns identified by the OIG and State's Foreign Service Grievance Board and whether they had been addressed. We determined whether State's responses had been incorporated into its operating procedures, policies, and supporting documentation by reviewing relevant agency documents. To determine whether procedural changes were consistently followed and appropriately documented, we reviewed relevant grievance files and selection board, performance standards board, and reconstituted board records—referred to as board reports. To determine whether additional notable concerns remain, we reviewed all 2011 and 2012 selection board reports, specifically these boards' written concerns and recommendations on how to improve the promotion process, as well as all grievances filed after the 2011 promotion cycle was completed, which were recorded by grievance staff as those related to promotion, low ranking, performance standards boards, or separation. We also administered an online data collection tool to members of the 2011 and 2012 selection boards, performance standards boards, and reconstituted boards to determine whether they had any concerns with the operations of their boards.

We conducted this performance audit from July 2012 to July 2013 in accordance with generally accepted government auditing standards. Those standards require that we plan and perform the audit to obtain sufficient, appropriate evidence to provide a reasonable basis for our findings and conclusions based on our audit objectives. We believe that the evidence obtained provides a reasonable basis for our findings and conclusions based on our audit objectives. Further details on our scope and methodology can be found in appendix I.

Background

State's Foreign Service promotion process is governed by the Foreign Affairs Manual (FAM), the Foreign Service Act, and the Procedural

Precepts for the Foreign Service Selection Boards—referred to as the procedural precepts.[2] The procedural precepts are negotiated each year between State and the American Foreign Service Association (AFSA)[3], and establish the scope, organization, and responsibilities of the Foreign Service selection boards that evaluate candidates for promotion. The procedural precepts cover areas such as the conditions for eligibility for promotion, guidance for boards on evaluating candidates, and the information boards are required to submit to the Director General of the Foreign Service and Director of Human Resources (Director General). The procedural precepts are provided to all selection board members at the convening of the boards and, according to State officials, are made available to all Foreign Service personnel worldwide.

The decision criteria for promotion in the Foreign Service, also known as the core precepts, provide the guidelines by which selection boards evaluate Foreign Service personnel for promotion. At least every 3 years, State and AFSA negotiate the core precepts. The core precepts define specific skills and levels of accomplishment expected at different grades and across the core competencies of Foreign Service personnel. These competencies include leadership skills, management skills, interpersonal skills, communication and foreign language skills, intellectual skills, and substantive knowledge—the skills, knowledge, and ability an employee applies to the job.

State's Foreign Service promotion system follows an up-or-out principle, under which failure to gain promotion to higher rank within a specified period in a single salary class leads to mandatory retirement for personnel in certain occupational categories. State's FAM outlines the time-in-class and time-in-service limits for specific occupational categories.[4]

---

[2]According to the Procedural Precepts for the 2012 Foreign Service Selection Boards, the regulatory language in the procedural precepts is considered governing if it varies from that in the *Foreign Affairs Manual* or *Foreign Affairs Handbook*.

[3]AFSA serves as the exclusive bargaining agent for Foreign Service personnel.

[4]Department of State, *Foreign Affairs Manual*, 3 FAM 6213.3.

Various offices and entities play key roles in the Foreign Service promotion process.

- HR, under the direction of the Director General, has authority over the Foreign Service promotion process.
- The Office of Performance Evaluation, within HR, manages the promotion process, including recommending selection board members and processing final promotion results and other selection board outcomes. The office also provides various types of assistance and services related to the promotion process, such as guidance to employees in preparing their evaluation materials and monitoring of selection board activities.
- Grievance staff, also within HR, process grievances relating to the Foreign Service promotion process or underlying performance information relied upon by the selection boards or performance standards boards.
- The Foreign Service Grievance Board provides an appeal mechanism for employees not satisfied with the outcome of grievances at the agency level. The board currently consists of 20 members. Each member, as well as the chairman, is appointed by the Secretary of State for a term of 2 years, subject to renewal.
- AFSA provides Foreign Service personnel guidance in preparing evaluation materials. In addition, AFSA attorneys provide assistance to staff who file a grievance with State or the Foreign Service Grievance Board.

The Foreign Service Promotion Process Includes Several Boards That Evaluate Promotion Candidates

State's Foreign Service promotion process includes several types of boards that evaluate and rank order candidates for promotion, identify other candidates for possible separation from the Service, and address promotion process-related grievances. Foreign Service selection boards identify certain candidates for promotion, "low rank"[5] others, and make other determinations. Performance standards boards then review low-ranked candidates for possible separation from the Service.[6] There are several mechanisms to resolve grievances relating to the promotion process, including through the convening of reconstituted boards.

Boards Evaluate Foreign Service Personnel for Promotion and Possible Separation

Selection Boards

State carries out several key steps prior to convening the Foreign Service selection boards. Selection boards then evaluate and rank order candidates for promotion. Next, HR officials process board outcomes before announcing promotions. Figure 1 provides information on key steps of the promotion process.

---

[5]The procedural precepts state that, with certain exceptions, selection boards are required to place 2 percent of assessed candidates in a given competition group in the low-rank category.

[6]The procedural precepts state that employees low-ranked by two different selection boards during a 5-year period in which the officer was rated by at least two different supervisors are administratively referred to a performance standards board. Selection boards can also directly refer an individual to a performance standards board, regardless of whether that individual has been previously low ranked.

Figure 1: Key Steps in Department of State's Foreign Service Promotion Process

Before selection boards convene	Selection boards convene	After selection boards convene

Before selection boards convene

- Department of State (State) determines the number of available promotion opportunities
- State Bureau of Human Resources (HR) officials designate selection board members
- HR presents official performance folders for all candidates to be reviewed by selection boards

Selection boards convene

Boards review candidate files and recommend candidates for promotion, mid-rank, or low-rank

After selection boards convene

Promotion

HR draws "cut line" on boards' ranked list of promotable candidates based on number of promotion slots → HR coordinates vetting of candidates above cut line with other State offices and determines which names should be removed from promotion list based on personnel changes → State announces promotions

Mid-rank   No further action

Low-rank

Low-ranked—and all other employees—have opportunity to file grievance with HR → HR convenes performance standards boards → Performance standards boards recommend to the Director General which employees should be counseled and which should be separated from the Foreign Service

Candidates recommended for separation have several options, including filing a grievance

Source: GAO analysis of State data.

Key Steps before Convening Selection Boards

State carries out several key steps before convening selection boards.

- The Director General determines the number of available promotion opportunities, evaluating factors including vacancies, estimated attrition, and projected staffing needs.
- HR designates selection board members. After the Director General determines how many and what type of boards are needed, HR seeks to fill the boards by soliciting volunteers and recruiting members to meet specific needs in terms of rank or work experience. Each board

typically has four to six members of the Foreign Service[7] along with a public, or non-State, member.[8] According to HR officials, public members can offer a different perspective than Foreign Service members, and can act as an additional safeguard over the integrity of the process. All selection board members must be approved by the Director General and cannot serve on a selection board for 2 consecutive years. Selection boards include generalist and specialist boards.[9] Once board members are chosen, State announces them in a cable sent to posts worldwide, which includes instructions on the conditions under which promotion candidates can request certain board members be recused from reviewing their file. Board members can also recuse themselves from evaluating a candidate if they believe they may be unable to render a fair and unbiased judgment.

- HR office of performance evaluation staff present official performance folders for each candidate eligible for promotion. The Employee Evaluation Report (EER) is a key document used by selection boards to evaluate candidates, and includes sections on the candidate's work requirements, performance, and areas for improvement. The EER is developed by the employee and the employee's designated rating and reviewing officers, and is screened by a review panel that is to provide feedback on any technical mistakes that should be corrected before the EER is formally submitted to the office of performance evaluation. The folder also includes information on the employee's training record and any commendations, official reprimands, or awards, among other information. Selection boards are to evaluate candidates based only

---

[7]According to the FAM, Foreign Service members of selection boards should, so far as possible, have a rank at least one class higher than that of the employees to be rated; have the depth and breadth of experience necessary to evaluate the employees designated for consideration by the boards; have a superior record of service; and have a reputation for unbiased judgment of personnel and for perceptive evaluation of performance. See 3 FAM 2326.1-2.

[8]According to the FAM, public members of selection boards should, so far as possible, have gained prominence in a profession, in business, in labor, or in a nongovernmental organization or institution serviced by, or having an interest in the Foreign Service; have some overseas experience; be available to serve on a full-time basis during the entire time that the boards are in session; and not be employed in the federal service. See 3 FAM 2326.1-2.

[9]Foreign Service generalists serve in one of five career tracks: consular, economic, management, political, or public diplomacy. Foreign Service specialists provide technical, support, or administrative services in 19 career categories that include positions such as doctors, office management specialists, diplomatic security agents, and human resource specialists, among others.

GAO-13-654 Foreign Affairs Management

on information in official performance folders, along with other employee records specified in the procedural precepts.

Selection Board Activities

Selection boards follow a series of steps to evaluate and rank order candidates for promotion and identify other candidates for possible separation from the Service.[10] The boards first screen all candidate files, and sort them into one of three categories: promotion, mid-rank, or low-rank. Those candidates mid-ranked are generally not reviewed again for promotion by that board. Next, each board member ranks each promotable candidate using a forced distribution scale of 1-10. Any time there is a discrepancy between board members of at least four points in the ranking of a given candidate, the members must discuss the case and, if the discussion results in any changes, adjust rankings accordingly to comply with the forced distribution requirement. Each board has a chairperson responsible for leading such discussions and helping to ensure that board procedures are followed.[11] Once all candidates have been considered and ranked by each board member, the board chair consolidates the scores for promotable candidates into one rank-order list. Once a final rank ordering is established, the board submits its final results as part of its official board report, which includes, among other elements:

- the rank-order list for each competition group of all candidates recommended for promotion;
- an alphabetical list of those mid-ranked;
- an alphabetical list of those low-ranked;
- an alphabetical list of any candidates referred directly to a performance standards board to be considered for possible separation; and
- recommendations concerning policies and procedures for subsequent boards and improvements to the performance evaluation system.

According to HR officials, the board report is the only document retained from each selection board. All other documents, such as notes and score

---

[10]Prior to the onset of board deliberations, HR trains members in selection board procedures and the roles and responsibilities of various parties involved in the process.

[11]In addition, each board has a designated advisor to facilitate operations and serve as an HR point of contact for board member questions or concerns.

sheets, are destroyed soon after the board's dismissal. HR officials explained that these documents are destroyed to encourage open and frank discussions and note-taking during the board sessions.

Key Steps to Process Selection Board Decisions

After receiving the selection boards' official reports, HR officials undertake several steps before announcing promotions. First, HR officials told us they draw a "cut-line" on selection boards' ranked lists of candidates recommended for promotion based on the number of available promotion slots. Then, HR officials coordinate the vetting of candidates ranked above the cut line with several entities, including the Office of Inspector General, the Office of Civil Rights, the Office of Employee Relations, the Bureau of Diplomatic Security, and the Office of the Legal Adviser. These offices respond indicating whether there are any outstanding issues concerning individual candidates, such as a pending investigation or other matter, that could lead to their removal from the promotion list.[12] In addition, in response to personnel changes, HR officials annotate the official board reports' rank-ordered lists of candidates recommended for promotion, indicating which candidates have been permanently removed and lowering the cut line accordingly. Next, according to HR officials, several staff, including the director of HR's Office of Performance Evaluation, review the revised list of candidates for promotion to ensure it accurately reflects changes due to vetting outcomes. State then publishes the list of promotions. Table 1 provides summary data for the 2011 and 2012 selection boards.

---

[12]Candidates can be temporarily removed for various reasons, such as due to an ongoing investigation, or permanently removed due to a change in personnel status, such as retirement or resignation. See 3 FAM 2327 and 3 FAM 2328.

Table 1: Summary Data for 2011 and 2012 Foreign Service Selection Boards

Year	Total number of boards	Total number of candidate files reviewed by boards[a]	Total number of employees promoted	Total number of employees low-ranked[b]
2011	19	8195	1465	94
2012	22	8560	1481	107

Source: GAO analysis of State data.

[a]The total number of candidate files reviewed includes some duplicates, as some candidates were reviewed by more than one board.

[b]Number of low-ranked employees is a State-provided number as of June 2013 and not the result of GAO analysis.

Performance Standards Boards

Performance standards boards convene each year to assess low-ranked candidates for possible separation from the Foreign Service. According to HR officials, there are typically two performance standards boards convened each year—one for generalists and one for specialists. Performance standards boards are governed by a set of procedural precepts outlined in the FAM.[13] The boards review each employee's file alongside no fewer than 10 randomly selected employee files from the same competition group and decide whether to recommend the employee for counseling or for separation. The board is required to submit a report to the Director General that includes a list of the members designated for separation along with individual statements justifying the board's findings in each case. In 2011, 11 employees were designated for separation by performance standards boards. In 2012, 14 employees were designated for separation.

Employees selected for separation from the Foreign Service have several remedial options. The Director General first sets a separation date. According to HR officials, employees can, until that date, choose to retire, if eligible; resign; grieve; or request a special review board, where the matter is adjudicated by a judge from outside the Department of State.

---

[13]Each performance standards board should include at least three members who, to the fullest extent possible, are all career members of the Foreign Service, are knowledgeable about the occupational requirements of the categories of the members they review, and are at least one level above those individuals under review. See 3 FAM 6214.2.

Grievance Process Based on Multiple Adjudication and Resolution Options

Foreign Service personnel have several options to seek relief through the grievance process in response to promotion-related matters.[14] Foreign Service personnel are encouraged to first attempt to resolve their concerns about their EERs with their supervisor at the post or bureau level. According to the director of State's grievance staff, State does not track the number of grievances that are resolved between employees and supervisors at post or the bureau. Employees can also formally submit a grievance in writing to the agency grievance staff, providing information such as the nature of the grievance, its effect, which law or regulation the grievant believes was violated, and any relief requested. Grievance staff process these submissions and, according to the director of the grievance staff, will grant interim relief from separation at the agency level, if requested. According to the director of State's grievance staff, grievances typically pertain to performance, discipline, or financial matters. Grievances relating to a low ranking typically pertain to the employee's EER, or alleged errors in applying the applicable precepts. For example, in certain cases employees have alleged that their EERs contained falsely prejudicial information, or that selection boards misapplied the procedural precepts in arriving at a decision to low rank a candidate.

Employees also have several options beyond the agency grievance staff. A member whose grievance is not resolved satisfactorily under the agency procedures described above can file an appeal with the Foreign Service Grievance Board no later than 60 days after receiving the agency decision. According to the director of the grievance staff, Foreign Service personnel can also file charges relating to prohibited personnel practices[15] via the Office of Special Counsel at any point in the process.[16]

---

[14] In most cases, grievances must be filed within 2 years of the occurrence causing it. See 3 FAM 4427.

[15] There are 13 prohibited personnel practices, such as discriminating against an employee or applicant based on race, color, religion, sex, national origin, age, handicapping condition, marital status, or political affiliation; or requesting or considering employment recommendations based on factors other than personal knowledge or records of job-related abilities or characteristics. These prohibited practices are defined and codified at 5 U.S.C. § 2302(b) .

[16] The U.S. Office of Special Counsel is an independent federal investigative and prosecutorial agency. Its primary mission is to safeguard the merit system by protecting federal employees and applicants from prohibited personnel practices.

Grievants may also appeal a decision of the Foreign Service Grievance Board by filing a complaint in federal district court.[17]

Reconstituted boards may be convened if HR officials or the Foreign Service Grievance Board determines a candidate was not properly reviewed or that the official performance folder contained incomplete or inaccurate documentation of performance.[18] In 2012, State initiated reconstituted boards in response to 16 grievances. The members of a reconstituted board are to be chosen, to the extent possible, on the same basis as members of the original selection board, and, to the extent applicable, are to observe the precepts and procedures for the original board. Reconstituted boards review, in addition to the employee under consideration, the files of the four individuals immediately above the cut line for promotion as designated in the final board report for the competition group and the files of three individuals immediately below the cut line. The reconstituted board rank orders the files under review from one to eight. If the employee for whom the board was reconstituted is ranked by the reconstituted board among the top four files, he or she will be considered ranked for promotion.

State Has Developed Procedural Changes to Address Identified Concerns with the Foreign Service Promotion Process

Prompted by concerns identified by the OIG and Foreign Service Grievance Board in 2010,[19] State took a number of actions to strengthen procedures governing selection boards and reconstituted boards. For example, in response to concerns identified by the OIG, State revised procedures governing the improper introduction of information about candidates and recusal requests. State also updated standard operating procedures for reconstituted boards in response to concerns raised by the OIG and Foreign Service Grievance Board. In addition, State initiated two other practices to strengthen safeguards over the promotion process.

---

[17]According to State, since January 2011, no State employee has filed a procedural complaint relating to State's Foreign Service promotion process through the Office of Special Counsel, and one State employee has filed such a complaint through the District Courts.

[18]Reconstituted boards are governed by a set of Standard Operating Procedures established by State in October 2011.

[19]Foreign Service Grievance Board, Record of Proceeding, FSGB 2008-051 (July 14, 2010).

New Board Member Oath

State developed a requirement that selection board members sign an oath in response to the OIG's concerns about the improper introduction of information about candidates during board deliberations. The OIG reported that it became aware of selection board members allegedly improperly removing documents from, or attempting to introduce information not already contained in, a candidate's record. In response, State implemented a requirement that each board member sign an oath to protect the confidentiality of board materials and report any improper introduction of information about a candidate. The oath also addresses board members' adherence to the procedural precepts and promotion criteria. A copy of each signed oath should be filed in the final board report.[20]

Revised Recusal Procedures

State revised its procedures governing candidate and board member recusal requests in response to OIG concerns about them. The OIG found the procedural precepts to be ambiguous regarding the allowable involvement by a selection board member who has voluntarily recused him- or herself from consideration of an individual candidate in other board deliberations, and also found the bases for recusal requests to be too limited. In response, State developed revised language covering selection board recusal requests, which was incorporated in the 2011 procedural precepts. The revised language broadened the circumstances under which an individual under review may request a board member's recusal. The revised precepts also describe the steps a board member should take to recuse him- or herself and make clear that, while this member will be excused from further consideration of the particular individual, the member will continue to participate in the other activities of the board.

---

[20]The oath reads: "I, _____ _____ (print name), do solemnly swear (or affirm) that I will perform the duties of a member of a Selection Board faithfully and to the best of my abilities; that I will adhere to the Precepts; that I will apply the Precepts and promotion criteria without prejudice or partiality; that any introduction into board deliberations of nonrecord material will be reported to the director of the Office of Performance Evaluation, and that I will not reveal to unauthorized persons any information concerning the personnel records used or the del berations and recommendations of the Board (so help me God)."

Updated Procedures for Reconstituted Boards

State updated its procedures for reconstituted boards in response to OIG and Foreign Service Grievance Board concerns about the operations of these boards. The OIG reported there was no regulation in place establishing the conditions that cause a reconstituted board to be formed, its membership, purpose, or the outcome of its recommendations. In addition, the Foreign Service Grievance Board found serious deficiencies and irregularities in the operation of six reconstituted boards, including destruction of underlying board records; inability of board members to confirm that the results reported in the final reports accurately reflected the board's decisions; evidence that the boards failed to incorporate the safeguards followed by regular selection boards; and lack of evidence that HR staff prepared board reports with sufficient attention to detail. In response, State negotiated and published updated standard operating procedures for reconstituted boards in October 2011. The updated procedures require documentation of steps associated with reconstituted boards. For example, the procedures call for HR to retain an official folder on each reconstituted board, which should include, among other items, documentation of the notification to employees of the names of board members; final board scoresheets that are signed or initialed by all board members; signed oaths;[21] recusal forms, if applicable; and the final board report, signed by all members or their proxy.

Renewed Emphasis on Certifying Board Results

State said it would place renewed emphasis on ensuring that all board members sign board results in response to an OIG concern regarding board result certification. The OIG reported that several former board members asserted that HR officials submitted to the Director General rank-ordered lists of candidates for promotion without those board members certifying the lists, or with results that differed from the members' recollections. State responded that, while a certification requirement, by signature and initials, of board results was already in place prior to the OIG's report, it would re-emphasize the need to ensure that this procedure is followed prior to remitting any board list to the Director General. An HR official noted that the use of proxy signatures for board members' certification of results was considered acceptable, so long as signed by another board member and not by an HR official.

---

[21]The language in the oath is the same as that for selection boards.

Discontinued Annotation of Promotion Lists	State reported it discontinued annotating promotion lists in response to the OIG's concern about this practice. The OIG reported that an existing practice of annotating candidate promotion lists—such as by computer, pen, or pencil—could be used to influence the board in favor of certain candidates, such as those who were nearly promoted in prior promotion cycles. According to HR officials, some HR staff had previously annotated promotion lists by noting employees who had the previous year received Meritorious Service Increases, which are given to some employees rank-ordered by selection boards but not promoted due to limited number of promotion opportunities. State reported that it ended this practice.
More Nonspecialists to Serve on Specialists Boards	State said it would try to increase the number of nonspecialists on specialist boards—which evaluate Foreign Service personnel who provide technical, support, or administrative services—in response to the OIG's concern about these boards' composition. The OIG reported that, since specialist board members are drawn from a smaller universe than generalist boards, there is a greater possibility these members will personally or by reputation know the candidates being reviewed. State responded that it endorsed the OIG's recommendation to include at least two nonspecialists on each specialist board. However, State noted that while it would seek to do so in the future, it needed to retain some flexibility to make exceptions in cases where two nonspecialists were not available.
New Procedural Manual for HR Staff	The OIG reported there was no consolidated procedural manual for training new HR employees. State developed such a manual and distributed copies to staff. The manual includes information on procedures relating to the promotion process.
Additional State-Initiated Practices to Strengthen Promotion Process Safeguards	In addition to State's actions taken in response to others' identified concerns about the promotion process, we found that State initiated two additional documentation practices to strengthen promotion process safeguards. The first is to have selection board members, in addition to signing final board results, initial each page of the promotable, mid-rank, and low-rank lists in official board reports, thereby attesting to the accurate rank order of all candidates the selection board evaluated. The second is to include selection board and reconstituted board member recusal memos in each final board report.

State Complied with Many Updated Procedures in 2011 and 2012, but Some Documentation Gaps Existed

We found that selection boards, performance standards boards, and reconstituted boards complied with many updated procedures in the 2011 and 2012 Foreign Service promotion cycles; however, some selection boards and reconstituted boards had documentation gaps for certain internal controls.[22] Our review of board files, related grievances filed since October 2011, and responses to an online data collection tool sent to 2011 and 2012 board members revealed limited concerns about the operations of some boards.

Selection Boards and Reconstituted Boards Had Some Documentation Gaps

Our review of 77 selection boards, performance standards boards, and reconstituted boards for the 2011 and 2012 promotion cycles found that board members and HR staff complied with many updated internal controls. For example, all 41 selection board reports we reviewed included a memo certifying final results signed by board members or by proxy, and documentation indicating that a public member served on the board. In addition, all 32 reconstituted board reports we reviewed included a statement describing the board's purpose, a notification to the employee of the board's composition, documentation indicating a public member served on the board, final board score sheets, and a final board report signed by all members or by proxy.

However, we found that some board reports, which constitute the master record of proceedings, had a number of documentation gaps. As shown in figure 2, there were several instances of missing oaths and incomplete documentation of recusals among the 41 selection boards we reviewed. For example, we found that 2012 selection board reports did not include 45 of 122 required signed oaths from members, or nearly 40 percent of the required total. Subsequent to our file review, State officials provided a portion of these missing oaths and other missing documents from ancillary records.

---

[22]We reviewed all selection and performance standards boards from the 2011 and 2012 promotion cycles, and all reconstituted boards held after October 2011, when State issued new standard operating procedures for these boards, through April 2013. In this report, we refer to all three types of boards as part of the 2011 and 2012 promotion cycles.

Figure 2: 2011 and 2012 Selection Board Compliance with Internal Controls

Internal control	Rate of compliance (Number of boards complying/ total number of boards)	Comments
Memo certifying final results signed by board members or by proxy.[a]	41/41 0 — 100 Percentage	
Signed oaths from all board members.	29/41 0 — 100	In 2011, there were 8 missing oaths involving 3 boards. In 2012, there were 45 missing oaths involving 9 boards. In several cases, oaths were missing from all members of a given board. State officials were unable to locate any of the missing 2011 oaths. State officials were able to locate 20 of the missing 2012 oaths in ancillary files.
Public member served on board.	41/41 0 — 100	
Promotable, mid-rank, and low-rank lists initialed by board members or by proxy.	27/41 0 — 100	In several cases, boards were missing a limited number of initials on some pages.
Board member recusal memos filed for all recusal requests.	36/41 0 — 100	In 2011, there were a total of 2 missing recusal memos from 1 board. In 2012, there were a total of 7 missing recusals from 4 boards. State officials were subsequently able to locate all 9 missing recusal memos in files outside of the board report.

■ Boards complying with internal control   □ Boards not complying with internal control

Source: GAO analysis of 2011 and 2012 selection board reports.

[a]The current director of HR's office of performance evaluation noted that proxy signatures by other board members are acceptable. All discussions of "proxy signatures" in this report refer to signatures by one board member on behalf of another board member.

We also checked for discrepancies between boards' rank-ordered promotion lists and official promotion announcements and found a total of 74 names recommended for promotion in 2011 and 2012 selection board reports that did not appear on corresponding promotion announcements. State officials explained that these individuals were not included on promotion lists due to requirements outlined in the FAM relating to the (1) permanent removal of names from promotion lists due to personnel actions such as retirement, and (2) temporary removal of names from promotion lists due to outcomes of the vetting process described earlier. State provided documentation to account for each removed name.

Compliance with procedures was better, but still not complete, for performance standards boards and reconstituted boards. For example, some reconstituted boards lacked final board score sheets that were signed or initialed by all members, and some lacked signed oaths from all board members. Compliance for performance standards boards and reconstituted boards is shown in figures 3 and 4.

Figure 3: 2011 and 2012 Performance Standards Board Compliance with Internal Controls

Internal control	Rate of compliance (Number of boards complying with internal control/ total number of boards)
Signed oaths from all members.	4/4 — 0 to 100 Percentage
List of all members designated for separation.	4/4 — 0 to 100
Individual statements justifying separation decisions.	4/4 — 0 to 100
Counseling statements for individuals not selected for separation.	4/4 — 0 to 100

Boards complying with internal control

Source: GAO analysis of 2011 and 2012 PSB records.

Figure 4: Reconstituted Board Compliance with Internal Controls from October 2011 to April 2013

Internal control	Rate of compliance (Number of boards complying/ total number of boards held from October 2011 to April 2013)	Comments
Statement describing purpose for reconstituted board.	32/32 — 0 to 100, Percentage	
Notification to employee of board composition.	32/32 — 0 to 100	
Final board scoresheet on file.	32/32 — 0 to 100	
Final board score sheet signed or initialed by all board members or by proxy.	20/32 — 0 to 100	In certain cases, boards judged as being not in compliance were missing a few signatures, initials, or proxies.
Signed oaths from all board members.	26/32 — 0 to 100	In total there were 21 missing oaths. State was able to locate 20 of these oaths which had been filed with the reports for several selection boards that had been asked to serve as a reconstituted board in addition to their normal duties.
Final board report signed by all members or by proxy.	32/32 — 0 to 100	
Public member served on board.	32/32 — 0 to 100	
Recusal memos on file.	1/1 — 0 to 100	Employee recusal request made for one board.

Boards complying with internal control   Boards not complying with internal control

Source: GAO analysis of reconstituted board records from October 2011 to April 2013.

Limited Concerns with Promotion Process Noted

Our review of board files, related grievances, and responses to an online data collection tool sent to board members revealed limited concerns about the operations of some boards. Our review of selection boards' observations about and recommendations for improving the promotion process revealed no concerns relating to the boards' ability to adhere to core and procedural precepts. Our grievance file review revealed one allegation of bias concerning a board member, which was not sustained. Our online tool revealed a limited number of procedural concerns pertaining to a few specific boards.

Selection Board Reports

The Director General requests that all selection boards provide observations about the promotion process and recommendations for improving it. Our review of the 41 selection boards' observations and recommendations revealed no reported concerns relating to the boards' ability to adhere to the core precepts and procedural precepts. However, we found that a number of boards provided observations and recommendations for improving the promotion process in several areas. For example, more than half of the 41 boards made observations and recommendations concerning the following:

- completeness, accuracy, or accessibility of the official performance folder;
- promotion criteria, policies, or related practices; and
- technological issues affecting board operations.

In addition, more than a third of the 41 boards made observations and recommendations concerning the following:

- uncertainty over how to interpret some performance appraisal information; and
- sufficiency or quality of promotion process guidance and training.

State's HR staff review and respond to board-identified issues each year and discuss proposed solutions with the Director General. In both 2011 and 2012, State issued worldwide cables with additional guidance to employees, raters, and review panel members to address key board-identified issues. For example, with regard to observations and recommendations about promotion criteria, policies, and related practices, the guidance stressed that candidates (and raters) need to demonstrate the extent of work experience within their "cone" and whether they are serving in "stretch" positions above their current grade level. In addition, in response to board feedback, State has developed a process, which was implemented in 2013, whereby employees can self-certify the accuracy of their eligibility for review and related performance information.

Grievance File Reviews

We reviewed all grievances related to 2011 and 2012 board actions and found that, with one exception, none alleged that any board or board member violated core integrity and fairness precepts such as the intentional introduction of extraneous material into the proceedings or overt bias toward an individual. The one exception was a case in which an employee alleged that a board member held a personal bias toward him and should have recused himself from considering the individual's file. According to State officials, this grievance was denied at the agency level in April 2013. Grievances generally focused on a complaint that a board misapplied a given precept in arriving at a low-ranking decision. For example, some grievants alleged that a board relied on comments made in the Area for Improvement section of the EER to support a low-ranking determination without corroborating evidence of poor performance elsewhere in the EER, as is required by the procedural precepts. We noted that HR officials often agreed with the grievant in low-ranking complaints and provided the requested relief of expunging the low-ranking statement from the employee's performance folder, along with related modifications to their "scorecard."

Online Data Collection Results

Our online data collection tool revealed a limited number of procedural concerns relating to the operations of three specific boards. Our online tool was designed to provide board members with an opportunity to identify whether they observed any actions, behaviors, or concerns that could have compromised their board's integrity and fairness. Our online tool was sent to 293 of 298 members who served on the 2011 and 2012 selection boards, 2011 and 2012 performance standards boards, and reconstituted boards since October 2011.[23] We received 206 completed forms.[24] From this total, two responses identified a total of four concerns with the operation of a board in 2011 or 2012. One response claimed that a board member had refused to follow precept instructions to consider candidate service in Afghanistan, Iraq, and Pakistan in a favorable light.[25]

---

[23]We were unable to obtain contact information for five members.

[24]We could not determine whether we received responses from 206 separate individuals because some board members responded anonymously. For more information, see appendix I.

[25]According to State, due to the scoring system, it is not possible for any single member of a board to make or block any board decision.

The same response noted that the board did not follow proper recusal procedures in all cases. The second response claimed that an "HR official" had inappropriately instructed a board member. The same response noted that the board did not follow proper recusal procedures in all cases. We obtained permission from one respondent to provide the respondent's two concerns to State's HR staff and the OIG for further review and follow-up as appropriate.

Conclusions

State's Foreign Service promotion process is conducted within the context of an up-or-out system and the practice of identifying a set percentage of staff each year for possible separation from the Service. Within an organizational culture that emphasizes performance and career advancement, safeguards to ensure the fairness and integrity of the promotion process are of particular importance. While we found that State had responded to previously identified concerns about its Foreign Service promotion process and taken a number of actions to strengthen internal controls over the process, documentation supporting the full implementation of these controls was sometimes missing. For example, we found that many selection board member oaths were missing from 2012 selection board reports and some boards did not include documentation of recusal requests. In the absence of a fully documented system of controls, there is a risk that intentional or unintentional failures to implement safeguards, by board members or HR staff, will go undetected and uncorrected. A failure to implement safeguards, in turn, increases the risk that promotion results could be intentionally or inadvertently compromised.

Recommendation for Executive Action

To improve and better document State's compliance with key safeguards governing the Foreign Service promotion process, we recommend that the Secretary of State instruct the Director General of the Foreign Service and Director of the Human Resources Office of Performance Evaluation to take steps to ensure that selection board, performance standards board, and reconstituted board reports are complete and fully document compliance with internal controls, including but not limited to signed oaths and recusal memos.

Agency Comments and Our Evaluation

We provided a draft of this report to State for its review and comment. State provided written comments, which are reprinted in appendix II. State concurred with our recommendation to ensure board reports are complete and fully documented. In particular, State noted that, during the course of our review, it examined areas we had brought to the department's attention, and made adjustments in procedures for filing signed oaths, recusal memos, and board reports. State added that it would continue to improve record-keeping in this regard. State also provided technical comments, which we have incorporated throughout this report as appropriate.

We are sending copies of this report to the appropriate congressional committees and the Secretary of State. In addition, the report is available at no charge on GAO's website at http://www.gao.gov.

If you or your staff have any questions about this report, please contact me at (202) 512-8980 or courtsm@gao.gov. Contact points for our Offices of Congressional Relations and Public Affairs may be found on the last page of this report. GAO staff who made major contributions to this report are listed in appendix III.

Michael J. Courts
Director, International Affairs and Trade

Appendix I: Objectives, Scope, and Methodology

This report examines (1) the Department of State's (State) process for ranking and promoting Foreign Service personnel, (2) procedural changes State has made to its Foreign Service promotion process in response to identified concerns, and (3) the extent to which updated procedures were consistently followed in 2011 and 2012 and whether any notable concerns about the promotion process remain.

To review State's process for ranking and promoting Foreign Service personnel, we reviewed relevant laws, regulations, and procedures governing State's promotion and grievance processes, including the Foreign Service Act of 1980, the Foreign Affairs Manual, the Procedural Precepts and Core Precepts for the 2012 Foreign Service Selection Boards, and the training and information materials provided to 2012 selection board members. To understand how these procedures are implemented in practice, we interviewed State officials within the Bureau of Human Resources (HR), including officials from the offices of performance evaluation and grievances. We also interviewed the president and several other officials from the American Foreign Service Association (AFSA), the exclusive bargaining agent for Foreign Service personnel, to understand AFSA's role in the promotion process. We interviewed four public, or non-State, members of selection boards, which evaluate and rank order candidates for promotion. We reviewed State data on the 2011 and 2012 Foreign Service promotion cycles, and the number, resolution, and status of grievances filed by candidates who were "low ranked" by selection boards in 2011 and 2012. We discussed with State officials how these promotion process and grievance-related data were collected and checked for accuracy. State HR officials told us the promotion data were compiled by HR's Office of Resource Management and Organizational Analysis. According to HR officials, HR staff members manually enter these data into a system referred to as the Board Maintenance Application. HR Office of Resource Management and Organizational Analysis staff members work with HR performance evaluation staff to verify the number of promotions, as well as the rankings of those promoted, and the number of those recommended for promotion but not promoted. These results are published annually, every spring. For grievance data, the director of State's grievance staff told us grievance staff obtained the names of every person low ranked or referred to a performance standards board in 2011 and 2012 from HR performance evaluation staff, then cross-checked those names against the names of individuals who had filed grievances. Grievance staff then manually searched the grievance files to determine whether the individuals' grievances involved low rankings, by year. We determined these data were sufficiently reliable for our purposes.

To review the procedural changes State has made to its Foreign Service promotion process in response to identified concerns, we focused on concerns identified since March 2010, when the State Office of Inspector General (OIG) issued its Report of Inspection, "Review of the Integrity and Fairness of the Foreign Service Selection Board Process." We also focused on State procedural changes made since March 2010. In addition to the OIG's report, we reviewed the record of proceedings for the Foreign Service Grievance Board's case 2008-051 from July 2010, which addressed concerns with State's procedures governing reconstituted boards, which are convened if it is determined a promotion candidate was not properly reviewed. We also reviewed Foreign Service personnel grievance cases related to the promotion process, from 2011 through February 2013. In particular, we reviewed those cases the grievance office had categorized as one of the following grievance types: promotion, low-ranking, performance standards boards (which review low-ranked candidates for possible separation), or separation. We selected these categories after reviewing a spreadsheet State provided that listed all filed grievances by category, as we determined they were most applicable to our review of the promotion process, compared with other categories such as discipline, financial, and leave restoration. We also reviewed all Foreign Service Grievance Board filings related to the same universe of filed grievance cases. In addition, we reviewed selection board recommendations to the Director General from the 2011 and 2012 promotion cycles, which we discuss further below. We also reviewed responses to our online data collection tool, discussed below, that was sent to 2011 and 2012 selection board, performance standards board, and reconstituted board members. To learn about State's procedural changes developed in response to the OIG's recommendations, we reviewed State and OIG documents showing actions taken by State to comply with the OIG's recommendations. We also interviewed State HR officials and officials from the OIG. To examine State actions taken in response to selection board member recommendations to the Director General, we reviewed HR summary memos and cables explaining suggested actions, and interviewed HR officials to discuss the status of these actions. We further discuss these actions in our report's third objective.

To review the extent to which updated procedures were consistently followed in 2011 and 2012, and whether any notable concerns about the process remain, we reviewed selection board and performance standards board records for 2011 and 2012 and reconstituted board records from October 2011 through April 2013. According to State officials, the official reports, referred to as board reports, from these boards are the only records retained; the remaining records are destroyed as a standard practice. We reviewed the three types of board reports within the following timeframes:

- All 41 selection boards reports from 2011 and 2012, the 2 years subsequent to the Inspector General's report, to enable us to assess the extent to which State had implemented and consistently followed changes made subsequent to that report. To ensure we reviewed the accurate universe of selection board reports, we compared the list of board reports provided against State cables announcing the results of the promotion process for 2011 and 2012, which also identified all boards convened in 2011 and 2012. This comparison identified no discrepancies.
- All four performance standards board reports from 2011 and 2012. There were two performance standards board reports each year for 2011 and 2012, contained within a single folder for each year. We received both reports for each year.
- All 32 board reports for reconstituted boards—convened in response to grievances pertaining to selection board promotion or low-ranking determinations, and convened after October 2011, when State issued new Standard Operating Procedures for these boards, through April 2013. To ensure we reviewed the accurate universe of reconstituted board files within this timeframe, we compared the files provided by State against an inventory list provided by State; identified several discrepancies and resolved them with HR officials; and presented a master list of reconstituted boards to State officials, who confirmed the list reflected all reconstituted boards relating to promotions within our requested timeframe. Near the conclusion of our engagement, we reviewed those reconstituted boards that had taken place following our initial file review.

To help conduct our review of the three types of boards, we developed a data collection instrument with data categories reflecting the information required and routinely captured in each type of report. To determine the data included in these reports, we reviewed applicable precepts and standard operating procedures outlining required information, reviewed a sample of the board reports, and discussed the reports with HR officials. The analysts discussed the data categories with two research methodologists and a senior manager and reached agreement on them before coding the reports. For all reports, two analysts reviewed each report jointly. Another independent party reviewed the results of this process after the fact.

To summarize and organize the selection boards' written recommendations or observations to the Director General, two analysts read and entered this information into the data collection instrument. In 41 selection board reports, the team identified 306 separate recommendations or observations. To analyze this written information, the two analysts developed a set of summary statements and higher-level categories to be used for reporting purposes. The summary statements provided a detailed explanation of the nature of the board recommendations or observations, including examples to illustrate what types of recommendations or observations would be coded under these statements. The higher-level categories served as abbreviated headings or titles of these more detailed statements. These statements and categories were based on an inductive exercise involving an in-depth reading and comparison of the board recommendations. The two analysts then tested these statements on an initial set of five board reports, by coding the text in them jointly. The statements and categories were developed iteratively, with modifications made as appropriate. The text was coded "yes" or "no." If a segment of text was coded as "yes," it indicated that the particular board had made one or more recommendation that fell into this category. If a recommendation addressed more than one of our categories, we coded it into all applicable categories. The analysts coded the remainder of the reports independently. Once concluded, the analysts met to discuss codes and reconcile disagreements as needed. The two analysts were able to reconcile all disagreements. A third party reviewer reviewed the team's work and provided several suggestions, informed by discussions with team members, on revisions to some of the categories to more clearly capture how the team defined and interpreted them. Final tallies of the analysis were obtained by counting, for each statement, the number of "yes" and "no" responses and reflecting the number of times a category of recommendation occurred in the 41 reports.

To determine whether State was following its procedures for promoting candidates recommended for promotion by selection boards, we reconciled selection board report lists of rank-ordered candidates for promotion against State official promotion announcements. We first identified discrepancies between the two lists by reviewing selection board rank-ordered promotion lists against the State promotion announcements. We provided a copy of our list of discrepancies to HR officials, who provided lists explaining the reasons why certain candidates were removed from promotion lists. Through this process, State accounted for all missing names. To corroborate State's explanation of why names were removed from promotion lists, we requested

documentation from State attesting to the reasons given for these
removals for a selected number of these individuals. State provided us
with this documentation, and therefore fully accounted for all
discrepancies between selection board report lists of rank-ordered
candidates for promotion against State official promotion announcements.

Similarly, we took steps to compare recusals we found documented in
selection board reports against State's master list of recusal requests. We
cross-referenced State's master list of recusal requests against the
recusals documented in board reports. Through this process, we
identified discrepancies, namely that four board reports had recusal
information that was not reflected in State's master list and that nine
recusal requests included in State's master list were not documented in
the board reports. We discussed and provided specific information on
these discrepancies with State officials. State subsequently presented
copies of the nine recusal requests that were not initially documented in
selection board reports.

To supplement our promotion process file review, we distributed an online
tool to allow selection board, performance standards board, and
reconstituted board members an opportunity to anonymously comment on
any actions, behaviors, or other concerns relating to the board on which
they served that they believed could have compromised the board's
integrity and fairness. The online tool's intended use was to gather any
information received from selection board members, and, to the extent
possible, follow up on any concerns or allegations; it was not intended to
present frequencies or tabulations based on the responses we received,
or to report comprehensively on the attitudes of board members on the
promotion process. We determined this type of online tool was
appropriate for this case because of the prior allegations of improper
behavior related to the process. Before distributing the online tool, we
shared it with three selection board members and incorporated their
comments, as appropriate. We also shared the online tool with State and
AFSA. We received comments from both State and AFSA; incorporated
some of their suggestions, as appropriate; and explained, where
applicable, why we did not incorporate certain other suggestions. We
requested that State provide us with email addresses for board members
from the following board types and within the following timeframes:
selection boards in 2011 and 2012, performance standards boards in
2011 and 2012, and reconstituted boards from October 2011 to February
2013, as we distributed the online tool in March 2013. State provided
email addresses for all but several of these names; we obtained some of
the missing email addresses through our own research and others from

AFSA. Through our own cross-referencing of State-provided lists of board members against our lists of boards and board members, we discovered that certain board member email addresses were missing. We requested that State provide email addresses for these names. Overall, we identified a universe of 298 individuals who served on the three types of boards within our specified timeframes. We were unable to contact five of these members for various reasons, including one retired board member for whom State had no email address, and several others due to missing or invalid e-mail addresses.

We sent an e-mail with a link to the online tool to 293 board members on March 11, 2013. Responses were accepted through April 7, 2013. We received 206 completed forms. We cannot report a response rate as it is possible that respondents submitted multiple forms or individuals responded who were not board members in 2011 or 2012. Board members could respond anonymously, and some respondents did not provide contact information. We reviewed written responses to identify any obvious or apparent duplicate or multiple entries, and identified one such entry. We reviewed all 206 completed forms and identified four responses indicating a concern or problem with the operation of a particular board. Two of these four responses constituted the one apparent duplicate entry, and pertained to a selection board convened in 2009, which is outside the scope of this engagement. We nonetheless provided this concern to State's HR staff and the OIG for further review and follow-up as appropriate. The remaining two responses, each of which identified two separate concerns, fell within our engagement's scope and are discussed in the body of the report. We obtained permission from one respondent to provide the respondent's two concerns to State's HR staff and the OIG for further review and follow-up as appropriate.

We conducted this performance audit from July 2012 to July 2013 in accordance with generally accepted government auditing standards. Those standards require that we plan and perform the audit to obtain sufficient, appropriate evidence to provide a reasonable basis for our findings and conclusions based on our audit objectives. We believe that the evidence obtained provides a reasonable basis for our findings and conclusions based on our audit objectives.

Appendix II: Comments from the Department of State

United States Department of State
Comptroller
P.O. Box 150008
Charleston, SC 29415-5008

Dr. Loren Yager
Managing Director
International Affairs and Trade
Government Accountability Office
441 G Street, N.W.
Washington, D.C. 20548-0001

Dear Dr. Yager:

We appreciate the opportunity to review your draft report, "FOREIGN AFFAIRS MANAGEMENT: State Department Has Strengthened Foreign Service Promotion Process Internal Controls, but Documentation Gaps Remain" GAO Job Code 320930.

The enclosed Department of State comments are provided for incorporation with this letter as an appendix to the final report.

If you have any questions concerning this response, please contact Bert Curtis, HR Policy Specialist, Bureau of Human Resources at (202) 647-2655.

Sincerely,

James L. Millette

cc: GAO – Michael J. Courts
DGHR – Linda Thomas-Greenfield
State/OIG – Evelyn Klemstine

Department of State Comments on GAO Draft Report

FOREIGN AFFAIRS MANAGEMENT: State Department Has Strengthened
Foreign Service Promotion Process Internal Controls, but Documentation
Gaps Remain
(GAO-13-654, GAO Code 320930)

The Department of State appreciates the opportunity to comment on the
Government Accountability Office's (GAO's) draft report on the Foreign Service
promotion process. We are particularly gratified that GAO acknowledged the
strengthened internal controls that we have implemented pursuant to
recommendations on improvements to the process made by our own Office of the
Inspector General in its 2010 review. As GAO reports here, that review concluded
that the process is fundamentally fair and trustworthy.

The GAO report clearly describes that the Department's promotion process is also
extremely complex, with over 8,000 employees reviewed annually by more than 20
promotion boards, meeting over the course of more than 12 weeks. The decisions
made in these meetings determine the future of careers in the State Department's
up-or-out Foreign Service personnel system. The required vetting of results with
the offices that handle investigations and disciplinary actions adds to the overall
complexity of the process.

The process is designed to be transparent to the maximum extent, while still
retaining privacy and confidentiality of decisions and, sometimes, the information
leading to those decisions. As GAO notes in Figure 4, due to the sensitive nature
of certain aspects of specific cases, records may be compartmentalized (i.e.,
retained in auxiliary files) to protect the privacy of the employee concerned.
Complete and secure record keeping allows the Department to look back on
decisions with the assurance that proper procedures were followed.

The State Department agrees with and takes seriously GAO's recommendation to
ensure that all our board reports are complete and fully documented, and that
signed oaths and recusal memos are filed appropriately. During the course of this
GAO review, we have examined those areas brought to our attention and have
made adjustments in our procedures for the filing of signed oaths, recusal
memoranda, and board reports. We will continue to improve our record-keeping in
this regard.

See Comment 1.

GAO Comment

The following is GAO's comment on the letter from the Department of State

1. This statement is incorrect. Although Figure 4 did note that State was able to locate some of the missing documentation in ancillary files, it did not note that this was due to the need to compartmentalize sensitive information.

Appendix III: GAO Contact and Staff Acknowledgments

GAO Contact	Michael J. Courts, (202) 512-8980 or courtsm@gao.gov
Staff Acknowledgments	In addition to the contact named above, Timothy J. DiNapoli (Director), Anthony Moran (Assistant Director), Joe Carney, Martin De Alteriis, Karen Deans, Etana Finkler, Ernie Jackson, Jill Lacey, Mike ten Kate, and Ramon Rodriguez made key contributions to this report.

GAO's Mission	The Government Accountability Office, the audit, evaluation, and investigative arm of Congress, exists to support Congress in meeting its constitutional responsibilities and to help improve the performance and accountability of the federal government for the American people. GAO examines the use of public funds; evaluates federal programs and policies; and provides analyses, recommendations, and other assistance to help Congress make informed oversight, policy, and funding decisions. GAO's commitment to good government is reflected in its core values of accountability, integrity, and reliability.
Obtaining Copies of GAO Reports and Testimony	The fastest and easiest way to obtain copies of GAO documents at no cost is through GAO's website (http://www.gao.gov). Each weekday afternoon, GAO posts on its website newly released reports, testimony, and correspondence. To have GAO e-mail you a list of newly posted products, go to http://www.gao.gov and select "E-mail Updates."
Order by Phone	The price of each GAO publication reflects GAO's actual cost of production and distribution and depends on the number of pages in the publication and whether the publication is printed in color or black and white. Pricing and ordering information is posted on GAO's website, http://www.gao.gov/ordering.htm.
	Place orders by calling (202) 512-6000, toll free (866) 801-7077, or TDD (202) 512-2537.
	Orders may be paid for using American Express, Discover Card, MasterCard, Visa, check, or money order. Call for additional information.
Connect with GAO	Connect with GAO on Facebook, Flickr, Twitter, and YouTube. Subscribe to our RSS Feeds or E-mail Updates. Listen to our Podcasts. Visit GAO on the web at www.gao.gov.
To Report Fraud, Waste, and Abuse in Federal Programs	Contact:
	Website: http://www.gao.gov/fraudnet/fraudnet.htm
	E-mail: fraudnet@gao.gov
	Automated answering system: (800) 424-5454 or (202) 512-7470
Congressional Relations	Katherine Siggerud, Managing Director, siggerudk@gao.gov, (202) 512-4400, U.S. Government Accountability Office, 441 G Street NW, Room 7125, Washington, DC 20548
Public Affairs	Chuck Young, Managing Director, youngc1@gao.gov, (202) 512-4800 U.S. Government Accountability Office, 441 G Street NW, Room 7149 Washington, DC 20548

Please Print on Recycled Paper.